# Roots and Wings:
## Gifts from Parents

by Charles C. Finn

authorHOUSE®

*AuthorHouse*™
*1663 Liberty Drive*
*Bloomington, IN 47403*
*www.authorhouse.com*
*Phone: 1-800-839-8640*

*Published by AuthorHouse   10/10/12*

*ISBN: 978-1-4772-6680-9 (sc)*
*ISBN: 978-1-4772-6679-3 (e)*

*We are never done with thinking about our parents.*
*–May Sarton*

# Table of Contents

*In memory*
*of the two people in all the world*
*most responsible for my grounding and my soaring*

# *Foreword*

Few things go deeper than relationships with parents, or are more complex. And as children become adults and their parents move inexorably towards decline and death, the complexity only deepens even as a primordial simplicity reemerges. Catching something of both the complexity and the simplicity in mere word-nets feels futile, yet I not only keep trying but feel emboldened to share some of these attempts with others. While these reflections are of course personal, they touch, I trust, on things universal. Many besides me have struggled with ambivalence towards their parents, and all of us, unless the natural order is reversed, have to live through the fiery crucible of our parents' dying.

The poems relating to my father—mostly written in 1988, between the discovery of his cancer in January and his death in September—are an attempt to "come to grips" with an imminent radical loss. Perhaps they can speak to others who have passed through the same crucible, or shudder to feel it coming.

While some of the poems about my mother similarly touch on her grappling with Night coming, many others address some of the intricacies of her and my relationship—at once wonderfully close and painfully distant, and not surprisingly at times contentious.

When worldviews at stark variance coexist within a family, they can't help but surface whenever matters of substance come up, which of course is often. The world has a way of intruding. As often as Mom and I agreed to avoid talking religion or politics, to stick instead to safe subjects like flowers, sports, poetry and Scrabble, we kept getting sucked back in. Our repeated failures to get the other to "see the light" invariably would lead to frustration if not anger, both of which concealed sadness at the gulf separating. Were these just matters of reason, we might have been able to have dispassionate discussions, but throw in mother-son, decades-long dynamics plus topics that don't lend themselves to dispassion, and it's clear that sustained detachment didn't have a chance.

Dad felt much as did Mom on matters religious and political but was better at dropping controversial subjects, or never bringing them up. This strategy kept us from "getting into it," but it also kept us non-communicative on important things. I grieved this distance between us long before his cancer.

All of this may be hard to fathom for those who have never parted from their parents' basic beliefs, or for those who, while differing greatly on issues, have been able to achieve a "live and let live" respectful tolerance allowing for honest exchanges that aren't taken personally. These poems speak, instead, to the painful reality of being closely bound to those who, in essential ways, inhabit what feels sometimes like a different universe and who see such difference as cause for reproach and lament.

But these decidedly are not poems of reproach and lament. They are rather poems of tribute and love—not the Hall Mark variety glossing over conflict but love poems nonetheless. Despite all the dynamics and differences, my parents and I shared a treasure world of memories and milestones and, most important, through it all we stayed connected, our bedrock heart attachment deepening to the end.

Come learn of the man from whom I learned stability, integrity, roots; come learn of the woman who opened me to beauty, empathy, wings. Ponder in the process whence might have come your own grounding and soaring.

Part I:   **Roots**

# How Good He Once Was

It is better for us both
that my father is no longer my hero.
In the early going a father needs to stand tall—
if not, what's a son to look up to?
But how can son come to accept
the darkness he finds deep within
as he grows from boy to man
if shadowless father never ceased in his eyes
to shine like the sun?
How good my father is no longer my hero,
and how good he once was.

*June 1987*

# Just So I Could Play

So much did my father want for me
the chance to play baseball in my budding years
that he took the trouble to organize a team—
rounded up boys to play and friends to coach,
searched for league to enter,
solicited sponsors for uniforms and equipment,
managed the team himself—
not so I'd be a star some day
but just so I could play.
You ponder with joy long after
how loved you were in your budding years.

*February 1988*

# When the Page Can't be Turned

"Dying of cancer"—
grim to read of,
must be awful,
powerless to stop the advance,
symptom-relief the most to hope for
and not always that,
cells malignant and voracious,
demise imminent.
To read of it you cringe sympathetically,
then turn the page.
But when it strikes too close
to escape by turning the page,
when it strikes, for instance, your father,
there it is facing you,
the grim and the awful,
and you begin discovering how consuming goes grief,
how deep goes love.

*February 1988*

# Really So Few?

In and out of my mind these days,
never far from my heart these days,
is news recently received from back home
that my father is dying.
I suppose the only way to come to grips
is not to run away.
It's not the building weight of it
so much as the occasional piercings—
what he is facing,
what we are losing.
How good there is yet time
to summon thankfulness for his thousandfold gifts
before bidding him adieu.
Can his months left for living
really be so few?

*February 1988*

# Either Way They Will be Poignant

My father, they say, is down to his final months.
Barely managing after Cathy,
how will Mom bear this?
The days ahead hold potential for blessing,
for breakthrough expressions of candor and caring,
but also for awkward silence,
for running from instead of flowing with.
Either way they will be poignant,
the days ahead.

*February 1988*

## Sacrificial

It has to be either a cruel universe,
indifferent and meaningless,
for spawning life that can only feed on life
necessitating incessant death,
or else a universe incorporating sacrifice
for not only survival but transcendence.
A materialist vision or a spiritual one,
that's what it comes down to.
The former sees in the latter a pathetic attempt at evasion,
a self-deluding escape from the inescapable,
while through the spiritual lens the materialist vision
seems bereft on an empty island.
No pretense at impartiality here,
particularly when the heart of me struggles
to fathom my father is dying.
Far closer than meaningless comes sacrificial.

*February 1988*

# May It Help to Hear

May it help,
as you gear up to take stock and leave,
to hear from tightening throats,
through rising tears,
how loved you are
by those with whom your spirit of integrity,
embodiment of responsibility,
steadfast caring
invincibly will remain.

*February 1988*

# *Bright Angel Waiting*

As you brace for the dark angel's descent,
remember the face of an angel of light
waiting in joy at the threshold
as can only a daughter for her father.

*February 1988*

## Two Songs Returning

I find myself remembering two songs
that moved me deeply in childhood—
"O Mine Papa," son to father gone,
and "Danny Boy," father to son gone.
Both pierce and lift the heart
of a son knowing beyond doubt that his father
soon will be gone.

*March 1988*

## Facing the Reddening West

I'm learning from Native Americans
to face west when I grieve,
its crimson sky announcing both savoring and sorrow—
gratitude for day's bounty received,
aching for day's glory receding.
All who know (therefore love) my father
face now, hearts savoring and sorrowing,
the reddening west.

*March 1988*

# *Incongruous*

Incongruous the singing of spring
when hearts are unsinging.

*March 1988*

## When Sitting with One Dying and Denying

When sitting with one dying and denying,
let us strive to be what is needed—
a presence available,
ready to speak if invited
but otherwise to abide with solicitude and silence.
A noble intention, to be sure,
but one quite hard to implement
when it's the father of your entire life
who's doing the dying and denying.

*March 1988*

## Both Less and More

My father is meeting his last spring.
Whether the forsythia shocks him with her beauty less or
        more
he chooses not to say.
For me the answer is decidedly less,
then with a stabbing decidedly more.

*March 1988*

# Hurry Serves Only to Bury

Denial variously comes.
The alcohol and drug variety
requires for dispelling a head-on collision,
a shaft of blinding light
to pierce the fog, penetrate the night.
No pain, no gain.
But something else entirely is the denial of grieving
where confronting disrespects.
Hurry serves only to bury,
and bury never finds healing.

*April 1988*

# Hard Getting Started

What first flashes to mind when searching his essence:
honest,
steady,
kind,
responsible,
gentle.
The deeper the respect,
the harder getting started.

*April 1988*

## Both Principled to the Core

I was reminded by a recent column in the paper
that Lincoln was anything but a popular president—
however acclaimed he is now,
he absolutely wasn't then.
We have something deeper than mere politician here—
melancholic undoubtedly
but manifestly compassionate and wise,
and if his actions, based on principle, cost him popularity,
well, there were more important things.
No wonder we look back with respect,
no wonder our esteem shades into love.
He calls to mind my father,
acquainted, too, with melancholy,
principled, too, to the core.
I'm having not a little difficulty
fathoming he's dying.

*May 1988*

# On Puns and My Father

Whoever says puns are the lowest form of humor
hasn't listened to my father
whose love of words has extended to playing on them
with imagination and fun
for as long as I can remember.
Even in this arid year of his dying,
puns from an inexhaustible spring
keep sparkling.

*June 1988*

*Always There*

Over the years
you've always been there
providing
quietly guiding
teaching values a boy to turn man
needed to know are possible:
integrity
responsibility
reliability
loyalty
love.
Father's Day seems right
for a boy turned man to say thank you
to the man who for the duration of his life
has always been there.

*June 1988*

# Is That So?

Dad's response upon learning of the death of a woman,
diagnosed the same time with the same disease as his,
was simply, "Is that so?"
He's always kept it in,
knows no other way.
You deal with what comes but you keep it to yourself,
never mind that you're dying.

*July 1988*

## Perhaps Where He Needs to Be

According to the ideal he's stuck—
no hope for acceptance and peace
if back and forth between denial and depression.
According to reality he's where he's at,
perhaps where he needs to be.
When it's your father who's dying, though,
the ideal keeps you praying for movement
towards theMecca of acceptance and peace.

*July 1988*

## This Time There's No Denying

Dad worsens.
Not quite "you'd better come" time,
but we're getting close.
He can't leave his room now—
breathing more labored,
panic more frequent.
A checkup tomorrow may signal more radiation,
but side effects would likely be fatal.
Subdued but steady Mom's voice told me all this.
This time there's no denying,
her husband and my father is dying.

*August 1988*

## Filling to the Brim

Lungs filling to the brim with fluid instead of air,
my father will go the way of gasping
until the last gasp comes up empty.
All we can do with sinking hearts
whether from next room or 400 miles
is to listen to his lungs' labored longing
for precious sweet air.

*August 1988*

# Give Us a Break

Three years ago it was Cathy—
same disease,
same time of year,
same hospital.
Then sister flower,
now father tower.
Give us a break, Dark Angel.
How are we to journey from grieving to healing
if you keep bringing more grieving?

*August 1988*

*Grounded*

Remembering Jesus addressing as Father
the bedrock ground of the cosmos
is comforting to one gratefully mindful
of his own 47-year-father-grounding.

*August 1988*

## Bond Unbreakable

Despite opinions often divergent,
feelings often unspoken,
across a lifetime has been forged between father and son
a bond unbreakable.

*August 1988*

## My Father Leaves Me Rich

One of my father's staunchest gifts
is his lifelong espousal of the ideal of honesty
and his lifelong effort to live it.
It hasn't always felt like a gift.
Back in my student days,
yielding to fears I stooped sometimes to cheat
which I could never rationalize away,
could never blithely dismiss,
for remembering this ideal of my father
which for all my behavior to the contrary
had become my own.
Regardless his material legacy,
for the likes of such treasure
as the ideal of honesty to aim at
my father leaves me rich.

*August 1988*

# Can It Be Time Already?

Ah, Earth, can it be time already
for you to fold back into yourself
the immensity of your gift of my father?
Can it be time already
for my eyes to yield jewels of sorrow
for the incomprehensible loss of him,
for my heart to bid adieu
to his towering kind presence?
A son knows it has to come,
the finality some day of his father's departing,
but can it be time already?

*August 1988*

## The Web for Us Life Has Been Weaving

Paying close attention to my mother and brother
not to mention my own heart
during my father's final days
not long after my sister's searing departing
tells me the web for us life has been weaving
is woven with grieving.

*August 1988*

## Some Such Welcoming

"Enter into the kingdom, good and faithful servant."
If my father doesn't hear some such welcoming
when he crosses the threshold returning to the Source,
then I've seriously misread the universe.

*August 1988*

## It Will Not Find Him Alone

We're where we need to be.
Thanks to morphine he's breathing quietly at last,
sleeping quietly at last.
With Mom and John home for the night,
tonight's vigil is mine.
However his final hour finds him,
it will not find him alone.

*August 1988*

# The Five of Us

We are all assembled—
the three of us bidding adieu
our eyes pooling pearls of sorrow,
Cathy waiting in the wings to welcome
(we can almost hear her singing),
Dad lying there set for departure
beyond communication of the sort we can hear.
The five of us come what may,
thanks to our destiny's gracing,
will find ourselves always assembled.

*September 1988*

*Miracle Gift from the Blue*

Watching and hearing Dad labor for breath
in the waning hours of his life,
then witnessing the absolute stillness
of his point of no return
from breathing out to breathing in,
crashed home the miracle gift from the blue
of every breath we breathe.

*September 1988*

# Burnishing

It was an austere but holy time
through which we stood together,
welded more deeply into family than ever,
steel coming out of the furnace of fire
burnishing with his memory.

*September 1988*

## May I Manage Something More

Would that I could have done something
to help him find peace in his dying.
Stoicism was as far as my father could manage
keeping feelings locked tight as he approached the end.
My sadness for what my father missed tasting
is perhaps less for him than for myself
if, my time coming, I manage only stoicism
with a taste for something more.

*September 1988*

# Mysteriously Enlarged

Intimation strongly has it
that one dearly loved and recently departed
is still in touch,
not only present but communicating.
But is there a qualitative difference
between how we can relate now
and the way we did then?
My curiosity is hardly detached.
Can he now understand,
or were the limits of comprehension present then
present still?
Am I able now to "talk" with my father
as, alas, we never could,
or is that just a wistful son's yearning
unwilling to be relinquished?
I opt for believing Dad sees the bigger picture now,
appreciates better his and my place in it,
which will have to make for a difference
in the quality of the presence between us.
Intimation strongly has it
that my life has just been mysteriously enlarged
by the passing of my father.

*September 1988*

# Beginnings

For Cathy it was August 1st,
for Dad September 1st.
That each chose a new month's beginning
to set sail on the dark sea,
to eagle-wing soar towards the rising sun,
perhaps was their way of reminding us—
standing bereft on the shore
losing sight of sail and wing—
not to take for endings beginnings.

*September 1988*

# Encircled

Little endears more than expressions of the heart—
eyes brimming,
embraces honoring the aching,
words that don't even try for not being able.
Sorrow seems an ocean boundless
until it finds itself,
feels the child of itself,
encircled by the arms of mother shore.
Arms of family and friends
encircle the ocean of our grief.

*September 1988*

# Beneficiary Yet

One of the achings over my father's passing
is knowing my daughter will grow up untutored
by the truthfulness and the gentleness,
the reliability and the whimsy,
of her Granddaddy
except insofar as these his dearest gifts
come to be so embedded in those he steadfastly loved,
like her daddy,
that those he in turn steadfastly loves,
like his daughter,
will be beneficiary yet
of her Granddaddy's dearest gifts.

*September 1988*

# Not Unlike Tears

Writing down words
when whelmed over by loss
could in part be cerebral escape
from feelings frozen as winter, arid as desert,
but if it is a dodge
it's straight into the dragon's lair—
stunned dwelling on the immensity
of spark gone from lifetime-loved eyes,
cold now and empty.
Ink can flow down cheeks of paper
not unlike tears.

*September 1988*

## Just to Hear the Two of Them

It's a Santa's face with hanging cord
ready if pulled to ho-ho maniacally.
Dad never tired of pulling.
Not usually one to let the boy out,
he did with this Santa,
whimsy bubbling into glee as he ho-hoed along.
You couldn't not laugh just to hear the two of them.
Mom faked dismay at how dreadful it all sounded
but clearly loved it.
I can't say I'm surprised to hear
this first Christmas without him
that she can't bear to bring out Santa,
but it saddens me to think what sounds she won't be hearing
that could soften exceeding sorrow towards healing.

*December 1988*

# How Painful It Must Have Been

"You're going to force me to become active"—
by this my father meant to protect impressionable girls
from his wayward son's influence.
He couldn't believe the school wanted me back after my
        travels,
to teach religion again no less,
after learning I had abandoned—for what he could not
        conceive—
the Church of my upbringing.
He never did intervene, that I am aware of,
but it strikes me now looking back
how painful it must have been for him
to worry about the welfare of immortal souls
under the influence of his wayward son.

*December 1988*

# Too Much Love to Keep His Grip

My uncle apologized for losing his grip,
for crying at my father's funeral.
I trust he heard gratitude from his brother's son
that he couldn't for the life of him,
for the love that welled in his heart
keep his grip.

*April 1989*

## Wishing I Had to Rack My Brain

It's my father's birthday.
I find myself wishing I had to rack my brain
about what to get him this year.

*September 1989*

## He Endures in Me

A son hopes after his father dies
to hold to his spirit.
Wherever else my father might be,
he endures in me.

*January 1990*

# Like Father, Like Son

My father, too, was into spirits—
the thought just struck as my eyes alighted
on three whiskey miniatures from his collection
on my altar of holy objects.
His was the business of distilling, then selling,
spirits fermented from corn mash.
Somehow there's a message here
for his son inclined to praise all manner of intoxication.
Kentucky bourbon his line,
Grail quest mine.

*November 1993*

Part II:  **Wings**

## Wisdom Born of Scars

No sooner had Baez quipped about our cowboy president
than mother left the room
with a parting, "I never *could* stand her."
It was great catching up on Joanie after all these years—
what questing spirit still
and gift to sing it!
Long has it dawned on mother and me (wisdom born of scars)
that we had best for the sake of domestic tranquility
steer clear of anything even remotely touching
on things political or religious.
Not that we always succeed (the world keeps intruding),
but thankfully tonight we did.
Guess whose singing was never discussed?

*April 1988*

# Even Were I Shorn of It

Mother is cute about my beard—
nearly twenty years now and her response is the same:
"Without that you'd look ten years younger."
It falls on deaf ears, her entreaty,
for I like how it looks—
woodsman gruff,
seadog wise,
soft for wife and daughter's stroking.
It may well announce my years—
salt and pepper is fast losing the pepper—
but even were I shorn of it,
it's doubtful my mother would find the face
of the boy she's looking for.

*May 1988*

# Consecration

A priest's fingers at the altar
holding up the consecrated host
as the faithful bow their heads
are not more devout with intention
or reverent with remembrance
than my mother's in this outdoor sanctuary
arranging flowers on my sister's grave
while hushed congregation of husband and son
bow their heads.

*June 1988*

# O No, Carroll

Young woman to man dying:
"Are you afraid of death?"
"O no, Carroll,
to be afraid of death would be to be afraid of being born.
If this life brought such miracle and wonder,
isn't it natural to expect the same from the next?"
Wise words regardless the source,
but what pride to learn today from my mother
they came from my grandfather!

*August 1988*

# Prayer of Two Sons Remaining

Sudden widowhood is overwhelming enough.
For it to follow so close on the heels
of the loss of her only daughter
makes life for an aging woman
feel no longer worth the fight.
Two sons remaining
pray their love and that of her friends
will bring to her darkness a measure of light
enough to keep up the fight.

*September 1988*

## A Tender Kind of Loving

When one endeared to your heart
carries depression into her declining years
not likely for its embeddedness to be lifted,
you learn a tender kind of loving
beyond the reach of preacher or shrink
that for the warmth of its embrace
offers even an enduring depression
something of a lift.

*November 1988*

# Respite from Combat

Mother to me during Scrabble:
"You make me so mad."
"Nobody can *make* you mad.
You're allowing yourself to be mad because of me."
"I'm allowing myself to be infuriated with you!"
We both laugh.

*February 1989*

## What I'd Best be About

I keep hoping she'll get past it, this paralyzing depression,
but can trying to hurry her help?
I'd best be about loving her where she is,
as she is,
lest my impatience with her give her good reason
to feel even more depressed.

*May 1989*

# My Mother is an Artist

Mother's care package arrived today—
animal band-aids for April and Adam
and baseball clippings for me,
exactly what each wanted.
Gift-giving truly is an art—
creativity grounded in care,
honed to a joy-bringing.
Joy indeed she brings,
my artist mother.

*August 1989*

## Dispense Then with Words

When one you deeply love
dreads death past capacity to be comforted by words,
dispense then with words
so her heart can yet find the comfort she longs for
in your gift of soft eyes and kind touch.

*October 1989*

# Hesitant Pen

I hesitate to write much about my mother
for all the ambiguity between us.
Besides she's still living
and would be sure to feel mortified to be on the receiving end
of what she'd consider a disloyal pen.

*December 1989*

## After My Father Stopped Breathing

After my father stopped breathing
and the three of us had time with him alone,
mother reached out to my brother, then to me,
(knowing our pain and our need)
and held us with suddenly strong arms.
It's like right away she assumed his strength,
did what he would do were she to have gone first,
be a support to his sons.
Many are my mother's gifts,
but none in my heart's memory stands out
more potent or more precious
than in that timeless moment when our world stood still
and her spirit stood tall
after my father stopped breathing.

*January 1990*

# When Words Can't Comfort

Mother's report back from the doctor
indicates "borderline anemia,"
with more tests ordered to ascertain why.
She's relieved to have a name now
for her oppressive lack of energy
but not yet relieved of an ocean of worry
as to the possible why.
When the two closest in all her world
slowly deteriorated
in spite of her prayers
before her eyes,
she can't not dread it is happening again,
this time to her.
Words can't always comfort
but love can always hold.

*February 1990*

## Cussing Will Have Opened the Way

For all her unfinished grieving,
Mother's not likely to make it to therapy.
Aware enough of the rage
held tight under the lid of her depression,
she's convinced spewing it out in a counselor's office
would just add shame to the furious pain.
But at least she's starting to cuss.
She's starting to blurt right out
words that used to horrify her.
You'd have to know my mother.
She keeps apologizing for becoming a guttermouth,
and what must we think of her to hear such,
but she can smile when we tease her
and admit how good it feels.
So she's making progress, my Mom.
What she can cuss out
maybe will be that much less stifled rage,
deadly depression,
to keep in.
If she ever makes it to healing,
cussing will have paved the way.

*February 1990*

# Be Slow to be an Authority on Aging

Few words can carry bitterness
more than "So these are the golden years."
Don't try, when you hear them, to convince to the contrary,
and for God's sake don't preach.
Allow the dignity of a point of view
formed likely over a lifetime
even if it imprisons in sorrow.
Be slow to be an authority on aging
until you get there.

*May 1990*

## Still Holding On

My handwriting makes mother feel a failure.
She takes it personally,
deems it somehow an affront that my barely discernible scrawl
is so utterly a departure from the neatness she once taught me.
What makes me think, talking penmanship or son,
she's still holding on?

*May 1990*

# It Very Well Could Be

Preliminary results of the bone marrow biopsy:
neither leukemia nor myeloma—
relief big-time as those were the biggest fears.
But then what?
How account for the anemia,
the terrible fatigue and loss of weight?
It very well could be, I tell my heart,
that my only mother in all the world
is dying.

*June 1990*

## She'll Have to Meet It Head On

Dad dealt with his dying by denying.
Mom's been through too much
what with his and Cathy's ordeals
for that to work with her.
In dread and bravery she'll have to meet
her own dragon head on.

*July 1990*

# *Firetheft*

Mother has decided to fight.
Since it's broken through with a harsh kindness
that she very likely is dying
and that denying it will leave undone
things only she can do,
she's stealing fire from the final dragon
to the cheering of her sons.

*July 1990*

## Think What It Says

Think what it says about someone
who never misses an occasion for giving,
who understands the smile when receiving a card,
the glow when opening a box wrapped with loving
containing a gift just right.
What it says
is we have here a heart a man blesses his life
to know is his mother's.

*September 1990*

## Home Gets Redefined As You Journey

Impassioned utterance to face expressionless—
it's like we were from different realms.
She asked how amidst prevailing decadence
I could possibly find reason to hope,
but when I began singing of my vision of Gaia
she wouldn't or couldn't hear.
Immediately she launched into a diatribe
against the anti-nuclear activists,
animal rights extremists,
and vegetarians who if given their way
will destroy the cattle industry!
I kept trying to hold up the image
of the resplendent jewel of the Great Mother of us
with her wounding and her plea,
but all she could manage was a begrudging
"It'll be a long time if ever coming."
I should have known better
to have a serious talk again with mother
on anything threatening to her religion or politics,
but how hard it is to give up on the hope
that lives so enmeshed by destiny
on matters fundamental might meet.
I smile to remember Quaker friends back in Virginia
both comprehending my passion and cheering my vision.
Home gets redefined as you journey.

*October 1990*

## Warning Unheeded

I crack my knuckles like crazy,
have done so, despite periodic efforts to stop, since 13.
Mother back then tried to scare me with threats
that my knuckles if I kept it up
would become big as golf balls.
I ruefully remember this warning unheeded
staring down at two sore and swollen.

*May 1991*

# Galactic Distance Separating

Indignant at the injustice to the whites,
she blasted busing as the root of public school problems.
I blasted back about separate but unequal
and, good God, what about *black* indignation
and over *centuries?*
Of course it accomplished nothing,
this momentary lapse from our avowed detachment,
but sometimes it's hard holding back.
When she switched the subject to the end of the world
saying others may think flood but she's convinced AIDS
(caused by you know who),
I managed to let it go its sad way,
musing yet again on the galactic distance
separating the orbits of this mother and son.

*August 1991*

# When the Sky Spreads Crimson

Beneath incessant worry and pervasive guilt,
bondage to propriety and bitterness towards aging,
politics far to the right and shoulders bent with grieving
are her legacies that will endure:
gift-giver without match,
sacrificial for her family,
passionate for her causes,
lover of words and their meanings, of poetry remembered
       sixty years,
inclined towards piety, bonded especially to Mary,
enamored of beauty with special flair for color —
in ornament and butterfly, in figurine and flower—
finding all her life in her beloved garden
the heaven she fears will elude her.
Enduring will be my mother's legacies
when the sky spreads crimson with the setting of her sun.

*August 1991*

# Familiar Territory

From recollections of futility we avoid talking politics,
but sometimes we can't help ourselves.
When Mom inveighed over the phone against Anita Hill
for destroying a good man's reputation,
I had to remind her of the 50% possibility
that just maybe this potential Supreme Court Justice
was lying through his judicious teeth.
For three seconds that stopped her,
but then she launched into the contemptible Democrats for
        putting her up to it,
the "women libbers" for supporting her blindly
in their frenzy to block Thomas' confirmation,
and soon back to poor Anita's fantasy life
that, along with political treachery, is probably at the root
        of it.
Back we were, my mother and I,
in that familiar territory of futility.

*October 1991*

# From Frying Pan into Fire

That my heart's pounding was sufficient to prevent sleep
gives a clue that the three hour exchange with my mother
was a humdinger.
We went and did it again,
jumped, despite our previous resolve, from the frying pan
        of politics
right into the fire of religion.
Time will tell if what comes from the sparks
beyond the sleepless night
is the customary burning
or just conceivably (it doesn't hurt to dream)
a glimmer of light.

*December 1991*

# Somehow Comforting

The prophecy that brother will be set against brother
and child against parent
is not what folks relish remembering from Jesus,
but somehow it's comforting to recall
when an attempt back home at constructive dialogue
once again has failed.

*December 1991*

# But if He Does Not Return Home

Should poetry of mine touching on religion
come to light some publishing day,
any pride my family might be inclined to feel
will swiftly be swallowed by dismay.
Catholics of the traditional stamp are chagrined
when one from the true path "falls away,"
unless, of course, the prodigal returns home
coming thankfully to his senses.
But if he does *not* return home
and then adds insult to injury by publishing poetry
that not only sings of his defection
but dares to reinterpret esteemed doctrines,
beyond forgivable waywardness what we have is betrayal.
Pride by dismay will swiftly be swallowed.

*June 1992*

## Comforting Reprieve

To say we both love flowers
barely scratches the surface.
For her they've been comfort and passion
to sustain her across a lifetime.
For me, suffused with her sensitivity,
they take away with their beauty my breath,
feed with their fragrance my soul,
stand forth each a living reenactment
of the resplendent Earth blossom.
For both of us ruing the chasm
created by world views worlds apart,
flowers are always a comforting reprieve.
Ah, to walk with my mother still
through the magical kingdom we both call her garden.

*June 1992*

# Facing Us Again

Mother's breathing is shortening,
advancing emphysema making the prognosis grim.
I'm reminded of the tremulous final minutes
of labored breathing of my sister and father,
of that awesome breathtaking silence
when finally into their lungs breathing out
no breath breathed back in.
We have this, my brother and I,
facing us again.

*July 1992*

## *Of No Mind to Hear*

When Mom brought up the inauguration,
I knew that disparagement was coming
but was surprised the target would be Maya.
She twice complained the poem was too long,
belittled its rock-river-tree triteness,
resented the inclusion in its litany of gays,
and was disgusted at Clinton's hypocrisy afterwards
for feigning it was a big deal.
When all this hit me within the span of a minute,
I could only manage, "Mom, there was substance there,"
which she was of no mind to hear.

*January 1993*

## Why I'm Drawn to Keep Reading About It

Mother seems edging towards full-fledged fundamentalism.
The rift between us beginning with Vatican II
has widened over three decades to a gulf.
Her referring to Limbaugh's bestseller as her Bible
tells you something.
Absence of toleration of difference
from apocalyptic fortress mentality
upon bedrock of scriptural inerrancy or papal infallibility
on behalf of the Only Truth
is what I consider fundamentalism.
I suppose why I'm drawn to keep reading about it
has not a little to do with my mother.

*January 1993*

# Whose Prayer?

When mother once again started railing
against the godless opposition to school prayer,
I asked whose prayer?
Would you as a Christian, I went on,
mind if intoned to your children every day
were Muslim or Hindu or Jewish prayers?
To her answer she'd not stand for it
and would send her kids elsewhere,
I responded but what if you couldn't?
She then said this is a Christian nation
and what did they come here for if not religion,
and I reminded her about an escape from religious tyranny
and our Founding Fathers' visionary insight
into the necessity of separating church and state
for the sake of *both* church and state.
We were talking, possibly even communicating,
but you wouldn't call it having a dialogue.
I was about to suggest my fondest hope
that kids actually be taught in public school
about the amazing extent to which a wealth of religions
has helped shape the spirit of America
(not, however, from the proselytizing perspective
of one deeming itself superior),
but knowing that would only have led
to further non-dialogue about the evils of relativism,
I decided to switch the subject instead.

*May 1993*

## Say Nothing

Having a mother ungracefully aging
(bitterness exceeded only by dread)
and having recently listened to heartening tapes
on the subject of conscious aging, of hopeful dying,
prompted me to consider mentioning when back home
that I had these tapes in case she was interested.
Wiser judgment counseled, "Say nothing."
You'd have to understand the history and dynamics
to appreciate my advance here.
Should she ever request, I have worlds to share,
but in the probably terminal meantime,
as I hope she'd respect my dying,
in sorrow and kindness I'll try to respect hers.

*May 1993*

## Think Mother, Think Gravity

Mothering: high calling to create from one's substance—
not just once, at birth,
but nurturing young life till it's sufficiently strong
to set forth on its own.
Then the mothering heart abiding its sorrow
blesses and lets go.
Think mother, think gravity—
fierce love's embrace,
generative dark womb,
sacrificial mothering night
inaugurating light!

*May 1993*

## Pensive Before a Picture

I'm sitting here in my study
pensive before a picture of a woman pregnant—
no awareness of camera,
just looking down thoughtful,
mind pondering, likely, a coming birth.
It's among my altar relics—
amethyst geode,
sower and dolphin carvings,
pewter eagle,
marble Buddha,
Dad's whiskey miniatures,
Cherokee vase,
owl incense burner,
obsidian dagger,
I Ching coins,
lotus candle,
assorted rocks, shells, feathers,
and a photo of a woman 52 years ago
about to give me birth.

*November 1993*

# Pondering Truth and Sorrow

Paging through *The Many Faces of Mary*—
with arresting pictures of statues of Mary
and touching words from the photographer-believer—
I thought what perfect Christmas gift for mother.
It got me thinking of my own views on Mary—
radically altered from my Catholic days—
and the sorrow when some day published
they will give to the likes of my mother.
Ah, truth may set free but not without sorrow.

*December 1993*

## No Greater Love

Could a son have greater love for his mother
than to hurry to the store to get batteries for her radio
in time for the Rush Limbaugh show
and then be willing to sit with her staunchly
and listen?

*May 1994*

## That Will Teach Me

Just when I give myself a pat on the back
for my filial sensitivity in carefully weeding out
from the packet of Christmas poems to my mother
those potentially offensive to her politics or religion,
I receive her call of dismay
over reference to body parts and cuss words
in two of my poems about Adam.
And then to hear her mortification
to learn I sent the same packet to her dearest nun friend
likely, she is convinced, to be terribly shocked.
That will teach me to get presumptuous
on the subject of filial sensitivity.
What a powerful, intricate, baffling thing
has existed the course of 53 years
between me and my mother.

*December 1994*

# *Legacy of Beauty*

A thing of beauty is a joy for ever:
Its loveliness increases; it will never
Pass into nothingness; but will keep
A bower quiet for us, and a sleep
Full of sweet dreams, and health, and quiet breathing.

I wanted to read this passage from Keats to you this morning for two reasons. First, it's one of the poems Mother memorized back in college sixty years ago and has loved to quote often since, as recently as her recent hospital stay. She was partial to the Romantics—she smiled to remember a teacher calling her "a Romantic rebel."

But the reason I wanted to read to you this particular passage is because it touches on what to me is her most striking gift: her love of beauty, and her creation of beauty. Whether it was the natural beauty of a flower or a butterfly, or the artistic beauty of an elegant piece of furniture or a delicate figurine, or the spirit beauty of the people she loved, so many of whom are here this morning—all these kinds of beauty and more her eyes saw and her heart went out to.

But not only did her heart respond to beauty, my mother *created* beauty. In her gardening, in her needlepoint, in her Christmas ornaments and vests and tree skirts, she made beautiful things. And in her lifelong love of people like you and me, she helped to make *us* beautiful. Some legacy of beauty Carroll Finn leaves behind. Maybe we can best pay our respects by finding more beauty, and by creating more beauty.

*December 30, 1995*

## About The Author

Finn spent ten years in the Society of Jesus after graduating from high school in Cincinnati. With degrees in literature and psychology from Chicago's Loyola University, he taught high school and then became a mental health counselor before relocating to Virginia with his wife in 1979. He lives near Fincastle with his family and commutes to nearby Roanoke where he is a licensed professional counselor.

Among Finn's writings is the internationally-known poem "Please Hear What I'm Not Saying." His published works, which can be found on his website (www.poetrybycharlescfinn.com), include the following:

Circle of Grace: In Praise of Months and Seasons
Natural Highs: An Invitation to Wonder
For the Mystically Inclined
Contemplatively Sweet: Slow-Down Poems to Ponder
Earthtalks: Conjectures on the Spirit Journey
The Elixir of Air: Unguessed Gifts of Addiction
Deep Joy, Steep Challenge: 365 Poems on Parenting
Earth Brother Jesus: Musings Free of Dogma
Embraced It Will Serve You: Encounters with Death
If a Child, Why Not a Cosmos? Lovesongs to Earth and
      Evolution
Fuel for War: Patriotic Entrancement
Earth Pleasures: Pets, Plants, Trees and Rain
Ithaca is the Journey: A Personal Odyssey
Steppingstones to the Civil War: Slavery Integral to Each

All of Finn's writings relate to the spirit journey. His own has been grounded in Catholicism and nourished by Jesuit, Taoist, Native American, Creation-Centered, and Quaker spiritualities.